MALIBU
UPSTAIRS / DOWNSTAIRS
AND OTHER STORIES

MARION & GIVEON CORNFIELD

AuthorHouse™ LLC
1663 Liberty Drive
Bloomington, IN 47403
www.authorhouse.com
Phone: 1-800-839-8640

Published by AuthorHouse 05/27/2014

ISBN: 978-1-4969-1553-5 (sc)
ISBN: 978-1-4969-1554-2 (e)

authorHOUSE®

TABLE OF CONTENTS

1. WHEELS

An out of control descent on my tricycle ended in a crash, with bits of gravel embedded in my knees and face. I survived, and graduated to a four-wheeled AUTO! This was all long, long ago, in faraway Dallas, Texas, but my fate was then inextricably wedded to wheels. When many years later I was able to voice my choice of a high school, I chose the only one in Tel Aviv that offered a course in auto mechanics. Montefiore Polytechnical Institute, as it was grandly named, was at an easy biking distance from home. But first, I must tell you how I got my first bike.

Buying a bicycle in wartime Palestine was of course out of the question. However, I spotted a discarded frame in an empty lot which I passed daily on my way to and from school. Also on my route there was a tiny bicycle repair shop. I dug out the rusty frame, which was half-buried under weeds and trash, and brought it over to the shop. Could it be resurrected? The shop owner was doubtful. But he had a suggestion: he needed help, so how about coming to work for a couple of hours after school? He couldn't pay me, but promised to help add parts to the frame from discards in the shop. I jumped at the offer, and in due course managed to assemble a heavy hybrid that was not easy to pedal, and which lacked proper brakes and other parts. But I had my own bike! I'll never forget the feeling of exhilaration that swept over me as I **rode it!** It was more intense than the joy I experienced a few years earlier, when my grandmother Bertha gave me my first pair of roller skates, when .I roamed the neighborhood pretending to be a detective pursuing dangerous criminals. That bike served me well for several years, during which I became a master bike repairer.

My first bike

At school I was an indifferent student, to put it charitably. What few courses I found interesting I followed avidly, but barely squeaked by in most others. Yet that was really of little import, because it was here that I met the love of my life. That's a big statement for a sixteen year-old to make, but it's true. Marion was one of three girls in my class, and it didn't take long for me to fall head over heels in love with her. It was a while before she even took notice of me, but things improved after I taught her to ride a bike. So you see - wheels were good to me.

After high school, I couldn't wait to join the RAF. Of course I entertained fantasies of flying, but it was late in the war, and I ended up in an engine repair squadron in Egypt, maintaining Liberators and such, that took part in the Italian campaign. When I was demobilized in June, 1946. I was twenty, felt very mature, and was ready to marry and settle down. No kidding. We had been going steady for four years. It would be no exaggeration to say that we grew up together. My parents would have preferred that I study medicine ("My Son the Doctor") or at least engineering, and put off marriage for some lengthy period. I would not even consider it: separate from my love? No way!

But first things first: we needed wheels to get around. So we pooled our meager resources and bought a pair of shiny, brand new bicycles.

Both bikes were soon stolen, within a few days of each other.

I got a job in the municipal garage, repairing dump trucks and the like, and obtained my driver's license. Both pairs of parents helped out, and we were married in November. It was a double wedding: Marion's sister Ruth married Menachem, a veteran of the Jewish Brigade. A childhood friend of Marion's was married to Yehuda Amit, who worked at the local Chevrolet agency. Through Yehuda, I got a better job there. I had bought an army surplus Norton motorcycle, a powerful machine upon which it was very tempting to "open up". Very soon I realized that this was too risky, so I traded down to a "Sachs Motor", a heavy kind of bicycle, assisted by a lawnmower-size engine. This was OK for the interim, but when we were expecting an addition to the family, it was time to buy a car. Now this may not sound like a big deal in today's terms, but believe me - it was a very big deal! And what we ended up with will really make you laugh. Still, it was a **car,** with four seats, even.

Our "car" (note right wheel)

It was a 1929 Austin Seven. It was so dilapidated that it elicited condescending smiles, which really hurt. But it ran, sort of. Most times. The battery was ancient, so the car had to be started with the crank, that protruded below the radiator. It had no parking brake (or any brakes to speak of), and a brick had to be placed under the front wheel, lest it roll away in a strong wind.

Across the road from the Chevrolet garage there was a small auto repair shop owned by Felix Burian, a nice fellow who was kind enough to let me park the Austin on his premises while I was at work. He also promised to have a look and see what improvements could be made to make it run better. One thing led to another, we became good friends, and when his partner fell ill, I borrowed some money and became "independent" - a business partner! Wow!

One of our customers owned a sporty-looking convertible, a late 1930s Czech-built Jawa, which was little more than a four-legged motorcycle. On this contraption, I taught Marion to drive...Next came a German-made 1938 Adler, our first "civilized" car that I purchased from one of our customers. This was the first car that I had reupholstered and painted (forest green). It was a four-door sedan, very low-slung, quite similar in appearance to the French Citroen. It was OK for city driving, but had an inefficient cooling system (no water pump), and hence a limited operating radius.

Feeling adventurous, I bought (for a ridiculously low price) a 1940s Humber that had served as a British army staff car. In its civilian incarnation, it suffered the misfortune of being parked too close to an exploding mortar round in the 1948 war. It was riddled like a sieve, and of course did not run. I had it towed to our garage, and after fixing the gas tank and radiator, managed to wake up the large 6 cylinder engine. It sounded promising, so I had the body shop next door fix all the holes in the body and paint it. That was premature: when I drove it, it handled like a ten-ton truck, and consumed gas like a Centurion tank. It also had very low oil pressure - a precancerous condition - so it had to go. So much for surplus bargains!

*****

By 1952, we needed a breather from the wars, austerity and the pressure-cooker atmosphere of Israel, and decided to move to Canada. Felix and I had a gentlemen's agreement, that after a couple of years in America, I'd return with modern equipment for the garage and resume our partnership. It took a while longer, but by 1956 I had accumulated enough tools of the trade and we - by then our daughter Eleanor was two years old - were making plans for our return. And then Mr. Nasser decided to attack Israel again, and the Suez War ensued. It was not a good time to go, everyone told us. We bought our first home, and only visited Israel periodically.

My duties while serving in the Israeli Air Force (1947-50) were motor vehicle oriented. I set up a repair shop at Headquarters in Jaffa, and also mobile mini-shops at various bases around the country - using tools from our own shop, which was shuttered. (Felix's army work centered on diesel fuel injectors that powered the IDF's tanks).

My idea for starting my own auto repair business in Montreal was to offer a mobile service at customers' homes. I was ahead of the times, evidently: such services now proliferate all over America, but at the time, I was unable to get the necessary permits. So I rented space at a large service station, whose owner shared in the income from repairs that I carried out for his clients.

I also equipped a mini-van and would go to the assistance of customers who were unable to start their frozen cars in the winter. The van's heater was useless, and I'd arrive at my destination half-frozen...

My shop on wheels

'36 Nash Coupe

I made a decent living, but never enjoyed the heavy, dirty work. In Israel it was pure torture to work in the sticky heat wearing coveralls, and Montreal was just too cold for comfort. My lifelong ambition had always been diametrically opposed to this kind of work: I wanted to make recordings. My workshop radio was probably the only one in Montreal tuned to a classical music station. So I sought connections, and ever so slowly, broke into the music field. It was ten years before I made the first move and took a job at a radio station, while keeping the repair shop as a backup. During this period, there were many cars in our lives. Salt sprayed on icy roads in winter was the great enemy of all cars in those days. It was not unusual to see low-mileage cars that had been exposed to a few Montreal winters rusting away at the edges, and undercoating did little to prevent it. We owned many, but never kept them long. I was well positioned to pick up bargains, such as a very clean, low-mileage 1952 Chevy with a broken transmission that I bought as-is for a song. Other memorable wheels we owned - in addition to a slew of DKWs, Nash Metropolitans, a very nice 1950 Ford, and a snazzy, leather-upholstered Humber sedan with automatic transmission.

We drove our 1962 Ford Falcon station wagon across the continent when we moved to Los Angeles in 1967. By this time, I was occupied fulltime (and a half) in record production. The firm that was distributing our Baroque Records in the U.S. imported me to head up their classical music division, which is what brought us there. It was also a good opportunity to round out my musical education.

*****

Ah, California - Car Heaven! The desert-like climate was the opposite of Montreal. Here, cars with 100,000 miles on the clock could still be completely rust-free. We gave Eitan the Falcon, and bought a couple of lovely Mustangs, a convertible and a coupe. It was in Los Angeles that we bought our first brand-new car: A Fiat Strada. A week after we got it, it blew a head-gasket, and it went downhill from there. We owned too many cars over the next twenty years to enumerate, but some stand out:

Marion's Fiatino - it looked better than it ran...

There was a 1947 Plymouth, purchased from a California Highway patrolman who drove it in the line of duty, babied it to excess, then bought it from the agency. The first car I rebuilt from the ground up was a 1952 Nash Metropolitan. That little car had been parked outdoors for I don't know how many years, and was baked to a crisp by the sun, yet mechanically, it was sound. I stripped it down to bare metal, inside and out. Marion helped with the upholstery, I had radial tires installed, and had it painted bright red and white. It was a great little car and became a landmark in Malibu, where we then lived. We used to travel and camp out frequently, but found our teardrop trailer a bit confining. Another project was a Dodge minivan that we converted into a camper, complete with kitchen, sink and icebox.

Our watch-dog Effendi guarding the van

The "Fleet"

Another car that went sour on us was a nearly-new VW Rabbit we bought for Marion's use. It was under-powered, did not handle well and overheated. One day, she was driving on the Ventura Freeway when a 16-wheeler truck tried to mount her, but only managed to push her onto the shoulder. It took the driver a quarter mile to stop his rig, when he came running up and swore that he never even saw the VW. His company paid to have it fixed, and we were glad to be rid of it.

The "Wascally Wabbit"

My tools (and I) were getting rusty, so I embarked upon an adventure, in the form of a major restoration. This was a derelict, sadly neglected 1929 Mercedes-Benz "Gazelle" cabriolet (a replica, of course). This had been grafted onto a Ford Pinto (shudder!) chassis and engine, but left outdoors in all weather. It was a back-breaking job, but what a payoff! I enjoyed this head-turner for a while, but it was not something to keep, since only I was able to (barely) drive it. But it fetched a nice price at auction.

My son Eitan inherited my addiction for wheels. He has a fondness for Volvos, as seen in this picture of one of his restorations.

FASTEN SEAT BELTS!

2. MAGEN DAVID ADOM

World War II was at its height, slowly moving closer to the Middle East. Due to the blackout, we had to get used to living in stifling homes with all windows closed and screened at night, and when car headlights were a mere T-slit. Thousands of young people over eighteen volunteered for service in the British armed forces, and in time formed the Jewish Brigade Group. One afternoon, Italian bombers came over Tel Aviv and attacked busy Ben Yehuda Street. I happened to be at my swim training at the nearby pool located in an orange grove. I had just dived in, and as I surfaced there was this terrible noise in my ears - I feared my eardrums had burst. Then I noticed everyone shouting and running to hide under the tress and understood what had happened.

At that time, *Magen David Adom* (the equivalent of the Red Cross) had posted notices all over town calling for volunteers. Actually, there was a big difference between these two organizations: the M.D.A. trained its volunteers to function as active paramedics, which is not the case in the U.S.A. Here I saw my chance to get close to the medical profession, which I was hoping to pursue. I went for an interview; the person behind the desk quietly sized me up and asked how old I was. I said fifteen (although I was a couple of months shy of that, and looked even younger). He smiled and asked if I was not aware that one had to be eighteen to join? I did not, but was determined to become a member anyway. I gave him many reasons why I thought I could do it and why he should make an exception in my case. He listened carefully, and I was accepted! His name was Nachtomi (everyone called him by his last name), and he became my chief instructor, and in time also became a friend.

This was an exciting period for me. Our training was excellent - beginning with an in-depth course in anatomy, then progressing into first-aid: Bandaging, splinting, transporting patients, recognizing symptoms, and so on. We also learned how to assist the physician on duty, accompanying the ambulance driver, and manning the old-fashioned telephone exchange. Our instructors were specialists in many branches of medicine, and I was truly inspired. I absorbed all this new knowledge quite easily, and being so young, became a kind of mascot of our group. When we became certified paramedics, we started our duties at the first-aid station, which was near the main hospital, though not a part of it.

Only those patients requiring immediate trauma care were brought directly to the hospital; all others were treated at the station. It did not take me long to get used to the hectic pace there. On Thursdays I was excused from school before noon to work at M.D.A. for the rest of the day. Our duties were never routine, whether we assisted in the emergency room or rode the ambulance, with sirens wailing. I had no problem getting used to seeing gaping wounds, bloody cuts and burn blisters. A very able physician was always on duty, and all I had to do was boil the instruments, hand him what he needed, support the patient and finish the bandaging. The usual casualties were mishaps at work or at home - cuts that needed to be stitched, burns to be cleaned and treated, fractured bones, sprains and the like. But there were other incidents that were unusual enough to be remembered. There was a young butcher with a deep gash in his hand - the cleaver had slipped. He was a Yemenite, as were his co-workers. Apparently it was their custom to stem the flow of blood by applying coffee grounds to wounds. It took quite a while to clean the mess before the wound could be stitched. Then there were cases of second- and third-degree burns that had been treated with cooking oil or melted butter.

There were quite a few drowning victims. The Mediterranean can be quite treacherous when stormy, and the undertow very powerful. British soldiers and policemen who were not familiar with it often drowned. I remember one of them, a very young man who we were not able to revive, and transferred to the hospital emergency room. A few hours later, while bringing someone else to the E.R., I saw the young soldier lying on a stretcher, his face was blue and he looked quite dead. He was hooked up to a respirator that pumped air into his lungs, making his chest rise and fall, producing a snoring sound. I never learned if he survived.

The popularity of stand-up paddling has recently soared across all oceans, but in pre-state Israel it had a long-standing history. The boards in those days were much larger and heavier, and were called *Khassakehs*. They were almost exclusively operated by lifeguards. Very few individuals could afford one, but my sister Ruth and I had a friend, Gershon, who did:

L to R: Gershon, Marion, Ruth

Unlike the single paddles now commonly used, these older boards employed regular, two-bladed ones, that did not require changing from left and right to stay on course. If a swimmer got into trouble, two lifeguards would hop onto the board, charge into the breaking surf and pull the victim aboard. Then they would turn around, careening into the crowd of swimmers shouting "Hatsida, Hatsida!" ("Out of the way!). Once , I did not get out of the way in time and was struck a glancing blow. I probably sustained a cracked rib, but was too embarrassed to admit it. It hurt for years...

3. Typhoid Ward*

By mid-morning I could hear the faint sounds of moaning. It began as a barely audible murmur, an as the day wore on grew into a sustained, heart-rending collective groan. The throbbing pain in my head got worse as my temperature rose towards noon. I guess that the sighs and moans were our only means to try and ease the pounding inside our skulls.

There were eight of us in the ward, four women on each side. Flat on our backs in white beds, black iron showing through the chipped paint. There were two large windows in the wall across from my bed, the branches of a huge jacaranda almost filling one of them.

With the soaring temperature my mind was playing tricks. At times I could not remember where I was and why; who were all these women around me; why was I so steeped in pain, my body writhing in agony and wet with perspiration. My tongue felt like a huge strange organ in my mouth, covered with slimy cotton-wool. I could no longer focus my eyes on the tree. The branches melted and swam together, turning into a tremendous, threatening wave crashing over me. Gasping for air I surfaced from my hallucination. I tried to keep my grip on reality, not to sink back into my nightmare. What was I doing here? What brought me to this place?

I arrived here by ambulance and was carried upstairs on a stretcher. It was two or three days ago--hard to remember. The Government Hospital for Contagious Diseases was located a few kilometers north-east of Tel-Aviv. In the spring of 1947 the British were trying in vain to hold on to their crumbling empire. This was the last year of the Mandate in Palestine, which was to become Israel in a few months.

The hospital had a very poor reputation in the community. We used to joke maliciously that the only way out once you were admitted was "feet first". Finding myself inside, I realized there might be some truth to this.

Days began early, with young Achmed, the Arab "sanitation worker" cleaning the floor. He carried a large pail of grayish water smelling of strong disinfectant into our ward.

He dipped his mop--a long handle with a filthy flour sack attached - and spread the water in long strokes over the floor. The night nurse would then make her last round and record our vital signs. Next came breakfast, consisting of some unidentifiable mush and warm milk with scum on top. I'd rather not mention the food. Even when I tried, I could keep down none of it. I just ignored it, since feeling as I did, even the finest delicacies could not tempt me. I was twenty years old, recently married, and slightly pregnant.

There were no antibiotics at the time, and no other medication was given. After a quick sponge bath, a kind nurse would rub our backs with alcohol, swab our parched mouth and lips and place a damp cloth on out throbbing foreheads. The Government doctor made the rounds of the wards every morning. He was a tall, heavy balding Englishman, totally uncommunicative. He never spoke to any of the 'native' patients, nor would he answer their questions.The head nurse, or 'Matron' accompanied him on the rounds. She was a middle-aged Englishwoman, short and plump in her starched white uniform and bonnet, rimless glasses in her round, rosy face. She would show him a patient's chart, and he'd grunt and move on to the next bed. Every Friday afternoon Matron took inventory. That meant that the few accessories from our night-stands had to be collected and counted before being returned. These treasures consisted of a chipped blue and white enamel cup for water, and a kidney-shaped dish for receiving our vomit. There were no bells at the beds. When one wanted water, or needed a bedpan, one had to call. Our voices were as weak as our tortured bodies, and even when they heard us, nurses were not quick to respond.

The days dragged on; another morning with Achmed and his stinking pail, another round by Doctor and Matron, another Friday inventory. When I felt up to it, I talked with Rachel in the bed next to mine. She was a young woman, the mother of a year-old daughter. She was worried--was her daughter being cared for properly, would she recognize her mother when she came home? Talking to her, I felt fortunate my unborn child was still with me.

Through the open window I could hear the chatter of the Arab washerwomen. Each morning they would squat in the shade of the jacaranda tree, washing the patients' soiled linen and towels. They began by starting a large wood fire under a huge cauldron which they would laboriously fill with a pail. From a large cake of soap they shaved chips into the cauldron, and sorted the linen while waiting for the brew to boil. They rinsed it to remove the worst filth, dumped the whole lot into the boiling suds, and stirred it with a long stick. Then they transferred the sheets one at a time into a galvanized tub, squatted on the ground and scrubbed them on washboards. Finally they'd hang them to dry in the sun.

We were completely isolated from the outside world. We received no visitors or letters, and of course no calls, as there were no telephones. Once in a while my husband would manage to bribe Achmed, who for a 'baksheesh' would slip me a note. How I treasured those little slips of paper! I could not respond; nothing could be taken out of our contaminated environment.

Across the aisle from me was a woman in her late thirties called Aviva. She was large and heavy, very loud and talkative. The nurses had a hard time washing her and changing her linen. As time went by, her hair began falling out--not that unusual with typhoid fever. She was terribly upset. One afternoon, Aviva was using the bedpan. She kept calling for a nurse to take it away--to no avail. Getting angrier by the minute, she yelled and cursed, her face red and sweaty. Then she actually did what she had threatened to do--she pulled the pan out from under her huge body and hurled it on the floor. A nurse came running, Matron close on her heels. Poor Aviva was chewed out like a naughty child, and Achmed came and dragged his wet rag over the mess.

The excitement died down, and we sank back into our 'normal' misery.

The following morning I turned my head to look at Rachel and ask her how she was feeling. She looked dazed and did not seem to hear me. I tried raising my voice, but got no response. During rounds that morning the doctor and nurses were whispering something I could not hear. Then they put a screen around her bed. She remained behind the screen that day, and that evening, bed and occupant were wheeled out of the ward. No one told us what happened, but we knew only too well we would not be seeing her again. I wept that night for the year old girl who had just become an orphan.

Up to that point I had been too ill and disoriented to give much thought to my own condition and that of my child--if there was to be any future for us. With Rachel gone and a new patient in her bed, I could hear a voice within me say: "Get out of here! Do whatever it takes to lick this thing. There is so much to live for. Beat the statistics!"

When the nurse came to wash me, I told her I'd try to do it myself. She raised her eyebrows, said nothing and helped me sit up. When she removed my gown, I stared at myself, or rather at what remained of my body I thought I knew so well, in disbelief. I could count all my ribs, and my legs were bones with knobby knees. All the horrors shown in concentration-camp newsreels flooded my mind. Is that how I really looked? Would I ever be my normal self again?

It was hard to be sitting for the first time after weeks on my back. I dipped the washcloth into the water, and my wedding band slipped off my bony finger. As I was trying to fish it out of the water, I felt something stir inside me--a reminder that I was carrying a new life. I put the ring firmly back on my finger, lay back on my pillow and smiled for the first time in weeks: I knew then that I--WE--were going to make it!

And we did!

This fall, we celebrated our son's 60th birthday!

* This chapter is a transcript of a short story I wrote several years ago for a contest sponsored by The Writers' Association and the Honolulu Advertiser; it won a prize.

4. EITAN

That was the name we gave our firstborn, and I believe it was well chosen. In Hebrew, *eitan* means solid, sturdy. Eitan is a not uncommon name in Israel; it can be a first name, but there are also many Israelis with Eitan as their family name, such as General Rafael Eytan. Be that as it may, *our* Eitan, having survived typhoid fever while in his mother's womb, most certainly had something good going for him. For our parents on both sides, he had the honor of being First Grandson; and that, if you know Jewish grandparents, is not small change!

He was a fast and eager learner, even before he could speak properly. He was only about ten months old when Marion happened to find a treasure at the greengrocer's: a whole nice red pepper! Store shelves in Israel, under siege in 1948, were bare most of the time: anything edible was snatched up immediately, so that pepper was destined to make soup for Eitan. After the soup was brewed and allowed to cool. As hungry as she was, she did not want to take any of it for herself. Eitan eagerly slurped a spoonful, and immediately made an unhappy face, spitting it out. "Kham!" he screamed (meaning HOT!). She checked again: the soup was *not* hot, but the pepper *was!* Of course she had no way of telling it was a hot chili-type pepper, even if it looked sweet and innocent...

When he was four and times were not much better, we decided to make use of my Canadian birthright. I went ahead to find an apartment and a job in Montreal; Marion & Eitan followed a couple of months later. They flew on a four-engine British Airways Constellation, a propeller-driven airplane. In mid-flight, Eitan who had the window seat, became very agitated when he noticed flames coming out of the farthest starboard engine, and as soon as the fire was out, and shouted that the propeller had stopped! A few minutes later, the captain's voice came over the P.A. system, announcing that "We have some engine trouble and will make an unscheduled stop in Keflavik, in Iceland. They landed safely, and were put up in a nice hotel, Eitan's first glimpse of the world outside Israel. Marion had her first taste of a coke, and has hated it ever since...

Safely arrived in Montreal, Marion was pleased with the apartment I had rented "in a nice Jewish neighborhood" following the advice of my mother's siblings, all of them old Montreal hands. Eitan was enrolled in a day school, and we began to settle in. This was not as easy as it sounds, since it was the dead of winter and we were not equipped to handle it. Eitan must have had a really tough time of it since he spoke no English, but at age four, it did not take him long to adjust. We soon moved to a larger apartment in the suburbs, and he was enrolled in grade school.

We were happy to learn that music was a part of the curriculum.. Given the choice of playing violin or 'cello, he chose the latter. In time his proficiency and fondness for the cello grew, and he joined the school orchestra and later participated in a European tour.

One of his classmates was Heinz Schlutz, whose mother was a teacher. They had a lot in common, and soon became good friends. When we acquired a television, the boys would watch it together, lying on the carpet in front of the set. A series of programs that aired at the time was called "Air Power". Heinz was German born, his father had served in the Luftwaffe, and I in the Royal Air Force... But that was all in the past, right? While watching an aerial battle scene, Heinz remarked: "I don't know who to root for..."

We made the acquaintance of Heinze's parents Ann and Werner, which soon grew into a close friendship. There was not the least bit of awkwardness, as far as we were concerned. We began to meet regularly and play recorder quartets, and during the summer went camping together on Cape Cod. The ladies got on 'like a house on fire'. By this time our daughter Ellie was old enough to be included in Eitan's activities, and the Schlutz's daughter Barbara, though a few years older, took Ellie under her wing. Once in a while, we'd drive down to New York for a few days, when our kids would stay with the Schlutzes. Truth to tell, we felt as close to them as if we were 'family'.

L to R: Charlotte, Denny, Eitan, Joseph

Throughout high school and McGill University, Eitan continued to play in various groups, and following graduation, joined orchestras in Halifax, Vancouver, and Haifa, Israel, then New Orleans. Finally, he joined the Canadian Broadcasting Corporation and became a program and recordings producer. That is where he met Denise, who was an announcer. The cello still occupies a place of honor in Eitan's life, via chamber music with friends, and the occasional orchestral gig. His wife Denny (Denise) is a gifted writer and veteran magazine editor. Daughter Charlotte is a musical Wunderkind - a terrific jazz drummer, though her real love is playing guitar and singing her own songs. "Kid" brother Joseph (they're both six-footers), having graduated from Concordia U. in Montreal, is promotion-oriented and full of ideas. To see Marion standing between those two giants is truly comical.

5. I Missed Him

In November of 1947, Britain's rule in Palestine had effectively ended. The UN had voted for partitioning the land, the British retreated to the port of Haifa, and Arabs and Jews took up positions, facing each other across no-man's land. Fresh out of military service, we were neither soldiers nor civilians. Under British martial law, the mere possession of any weapon could result in a hanging. We in the *Hagana* manned pillboxes hastily erected under cover of darkness, two men to a position. Our equipment consisted of a WWI vintage Lee Enfield rifle with five rounds, but our 'serious' firepower was a Sten Gun and two clips of ammunition. In addition, we were issued a grenade apiece, to be used only after our last round was spent, rather than fall alive into Arab hands.

Dodging sniper fire from the top of a mosque overlooking Tel Aviv, we dashed across deserted alleyways and made it to our pillbox. My partner that night was a veteran, a man in his thirties called Arnold. A new immigrant, he spoke a mixture of his native Polish and a smattering of Hebrew and Yiddish. He had fought in the Spanish civil war, and spent WWII as a partisan, living in the frozen forests of Poland. After hearing his story, I felt my own service in the Royal Air Force looked like a cakewalk.

I peeled an orange, broke it in half and offered it to Arnold. Although we had only met a few hours earlier, I felt as if I had known him for years. There was an air of quiet confidence about him, and a comfortable camaraderie, as we spoke in whispers. Time lay heavy on our hands, and it was not yet midnight. The clouds that had earlier hidden the moon now dispersed, and everything about us was bathed in a bright, silvery light. We took turns peering out of the brick-sized apertures of our pillbox; nothing but garbage, rubble and half-ruined houses out there...

Suddenly I felt the skin on the back of neck crawling: across the empty space between us, I could see a man, rifle in hand, walking in a crouch. My first reaction was of annoyance: The idiot! I thought. What's he doing out there in the full moonlight? Did he think that if he walked like Groucho Marx he'd be less visible?

But this was an armed Arab, *my enemy*, who would not hesitate to kill me. It was my duty to stop him. I nudged Arnold, whispering as I pulled back the safety-catch on my Sten gun: Look! There! See him?

Arnold tensed and raised his rifle, but it could not be aimed effectively from inside the pillbox. I wanted to shout, to warn the man away, *remove him from my sight!*

Get him! Arnold hissed. I swallowed hard, pointed the Sten gun, and squeezed the trigger.

The gun, reputedly one of the most unreliable weapons of WWII, did not disappoint: it fired a single round, instead of the rapid fire I expected. The man straightened up, wheeled about, and ran full tilt, crashing into the shadows.

I had missed him.

And I was glad.

6. DOCTOR TICHO

One morning after dropping off my son at his day care center I went for a swim. I dove into the pool, and when I came up for air I noticed a little smudge in my eye, which did not realy bother me. I finished my workout, and still this tiny obstruction was in the same spot, although I did not feel any discomfort. I could have easily ignored it, but fortunately decided to pay a visit to an ophthalmologist anyway. As I sat in the examination room, his expression slowly changed and he seemed concerned. He darkened the room and focused tiny, concentrated rays of light into my eye, checking it from every angle. He never said a word, and I was beginning to feel uneasy. When he was done, he turned the light back on and solemnly told me what he found: a detachment of the retina. He explained how serious this condition was, which if not treated promptly, would result in my losing vision in that eye. The treatment was no simple matter. In all of Israel there was only one man who could help me - the only ophthalmologist who had mastered the procedure for operating on detached retinas and 'weld' them back into place. Dr. Ticho practiced in Jerusalem, and I would have to go there at once, preferably today! I was stunned and totally unprepared to drop everything and go to Jerusalem. I walked back to my parents' home where I had left Eitan, and carefully told them what had happened. That evening, when Giv came to pick us up and heard the news, he drove us home, brought Eitan's crib and clothes to my parents', and I got ready to be away from home for quite some time.

The following morning I boarded a bus to Jerusalem. I had no idea who Dr. Ticho was, I did not know what his clinic was like - I just knew he was the only person able to help me. The road up into the Judean hills was a bleak sight. Nearing Jerusalem, burned-out remains of armored trucks lined the side of the highway, a solemn reminder of the fate of their occupants who had perished trying to keep up the flow of supplies to the beleaguered city during the war.

I arrived at the clinic, a compound consisting of two buildings: one was the Tichos' residential villa - a very nice one indeed - the other a plain structure with a waiting room, examination rooms, operating theatre, administration office, several rooms for in-patients, and last but not least - an outhouse! There was quite a crowd in the waiting room. Most patients never got to see Dr. Ticho; his assistants took care of them. After a long wait, I was called into his office. A short, friendly elderly man greeted me from behind his desk. His blue eyes had a sparkle, and his manner was businesslike and to the point. Again my eye was scrutinized from all angles, and he told me very frankly what to expect. He would perform the surgery the following morning. I would then have to spend three weeks on my back with both eyes bandaged, and after that, two more weeks of wearing special opaque glasses with tiny pin-points in the center. The rate of success - about fifty percent, possibly slightly higher because I was so young,

After Dr. Ticho and his assistants were done with their tests, I was led by a nurse to the room which was to become my home for the next three weeks. Both eyes were bandaged right away, to keep them still and relaxed. I managed to get a good look at my surroundings before darkness descended. It was a medium-sized room, with a tall window overlooking the courtyard. The bed under the window was occupied by an elderly woman who had undergone the same type of surgery a few days earlier. She was uncommunicative, muttering to herself and moaning most of the time. Next to the door was a crib with a three-year old girl who needed strabismus surgery. My bed stood against the opposite wall. From that point on I was left to myself, with my thoughts and misgivings, which were numerous. No one to talk to, nothing to see or hear, other than some noisy crows outside. The outhouse was close to the room, a fact I could not ignore, even with my bandaged eyes.

The next morning I was taken to the operating room. I had time to look around before the procedure began. It was a green-tiled, fairly large room. I was placed on the operating table and a nurse strapped down my arms. Beside Dr. Ticho was his assistant, a huge Hungarian fellow, whom I immediately named "The Big Stiff". He looked like a butcher and walked around like a prizefighter. There were also two nurses. The procedure was more or less explained to me (I insisted that they do so). Since my cooperation was necessary during the surgery, a local anesthetic would be administered. The painkilling injections proved to be less than effective. My healthy eye was covered, and saline solution was dripping into the other one, which was then clamped open. Being awake, I was determined to learn as much as I could about the method. All I could see now was a bright red blob where my eye was supposed to be, and all I could do was to listen carefully to what was said. I felt a scalpel snipping a muscle around the eyeball, then another. I was in physical and emotional agony. The voices around me sounded calm - routine comments that are used in all operating rooms. It seemed like an eternity before they were ready to proceed with the actual 'welding' of the retina. At the time it was done with diathermy (the laser had not been dreamed of) - a method of applying heat by means of high-frequency electric current. Finally the sutures were put in place, bandages applied, and the ordeal was over. It had taken just under three hours. I was wheeled back into my room, placed flat on my back with a stern warning to not move my head. I was drained and exhausted, wishing I could turn over on my side and go to sleep...

Dr. Abraham Ticho was a well-known ophthalmologist whose fame had spread beyond the Middle East. His main field of expertise was the treatment of tropical diseases of the eye, especially trachoma. But he was just as adept in complicated surgical procedures, including the detached retina. Even better known than the doctor was his wife Anna, whose drawings - mostly views of Jerusalem - are prominently displayed in many museums. He was seventy years old when I met him, his capable hands rock-steady.

I did not sleep at all the night after the surgery, for fear of moving my head or turning on my side. Slowly I began to get used to my awkward position, however reluctantly. In 1950 water in Jerusalem was still in very short supply and severely rationed. The clinic conserved its water by giving their patients one sponge bath per week, and of course there was the outhouse for ambulatory patients and their visitors. It was spring, with its typical early heat waves. My bed got soaked with perspiration and my back became glued to the mattress. To top it off, no sponge-bath until Friday, in honor of the Sabbath. I was not able to feed myself and had to be fed by a nurse. A thick slab of bread for a sandwich - my mouth could not open wide enough to bite into it, my whole face was much too sore. For drinking we could choose between evil-smelling water or tea. We understood, though - there was the matter of austerity, food was scarce and nobody expected any luxuries. Even toilet tissue was unavailable, a true problem in our situation. The worst was being confined to my bed blindfolded, relying solely on my hearing to know what was going on around me, identifying the persons who took care of me by their voices. Giv could only come to see me on Saturdays - what a welcome break from the monotony of the interminable week. Our car - an old Adler - could barely make it up the steep road to Jerusalem, with many stops to take care of the boiling radiator. He brought with him some cherished gifts: bottled orange juice, toilet paper, and best of all - a small radio for my bedside. My elation was not very long-lived. The night nurse, whom I had never seen, an immigrant from Rumania who spoke very little Hebrew, came quietly into our room to check on her patients. Assuming that I was asleep, she helped herself to the juice and generous amounts of the precious paper, a habit she repeated every night. There was nothing I could say - I still had to depend on her help for a while. Then there was Mr. Halaban, the administrator, a tiny powerhouse of a bureaucrat. When he heard about my radio, he stormed into the room, outraged at my nerve to use so much electricity! After much pleading and my promise to pay my share of the electric bill, I was permitted to keep it. I also managed to make a deal with the head nurse to give me a quickie bath in the mornings - she too was paid for her generosity.

One morning there was a big commotion in the yard. I heard a number of cars arriving at the clinic and a babble of excited voices. I found out later that it was Madame Chiang-Kai-Shek who had come with her entourage for a check-up. She had been a patient of Dr. Ticho for many years.

I believe those were the longest three weeks of my life, but finally the day arrived when my bandages were removed. The light seemed so bright I could barely squint, but my vision was intact! Dr. Ticho and 'The Big Stiff' examined the eye carefully and pronounced their handiwork a success. I was given black, opaque glasses with tiny pin-points in their centers and had to get used to seeing the world through a very narrow tunnel. I was quite dizzy sitting up for the first time, but getting up was worse: my muscles were atrophied and I had lost my sense of balance. It took me a while to get used to the real world.

I had one last session in Dr. Ticho's office, with detailed instructions about care in the future. My days of vigorous physical activity were over - a serious blow. No bending, no lifting, no swimming for a long time yet. The burning question was: What about having another child? He pondered this for a while, then said he thought it might be possible if I waited at least three years, and had special supervision during the delivery. I was not too happy to hear this: Eitan was two an a half years old and I thought it was time to present him with a sibling. The more pressing problem - how do you take care of a little boy without ever lifting him?

Giv took me home, and necessity made a good teacher: I learned how to take care of Eitan without having to carry him. I learned to pick up objects from the floor with my feet (at which I am still quite adept), and I got used to the idea of gentle activities and avoiding falls. That eliminated skiing from any future plans.

On a trip to Israel a few years ago, we visited the Ticho Museum, named in honor of his artist wife Anna, whose works are beautifully displayed in their former home. Dr. Ticho's huge operating room had become an upscale restaurant, where we enjoyed a delicious lunch amid the many works of this gifted artist.

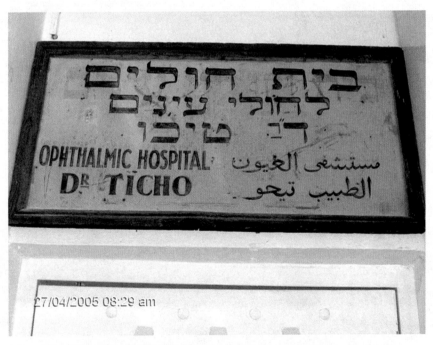

Original sign above the hospital entrance

This episode is long and detailed, but there were two reasons for my verbosity. First, it was a major turning point in my life. Secondly, I wanted to present a picture of retina surgery in its infancy over half a century ago, compared to the vast improvements available today. In my case, there were many more surgical interventions through the years to save my vision, about which I will not elaborate. Suffice it to say that I have been extremely fortunate to have found the most outstanding specialists in the field. Ophthalmology has come out of the dark ages - research is ongoing, making giant strides. To this day I have never taken my vision for granted: every time I thread a needle on the first try. I feel elated - and being able to drive easily at night never fails to remind me how fortunate I am. Today, over half a century later, the vision in that eye is 20/20!!

7. WALKING ON AIR

The year was 1946, when tens of thousands of servicemen and women who had served in His Majesty's Forces in the war were discharged. There were only so many jobs to be had, and competition was fierce. There were shortages of just about everything - far worse than had been the case during the war years. This resulted in a high rate of unemployment, and I was very anxious to find work and realize my dream of marrying my high school sweetheart. We had been 'going steady' for four years, and both of us felt quite mature and ready to start our life together.

As an aircraft engine mechanic in the Royal Air Force, I felt entitled to lay claim to a certain expertise, and so applied to several workshops in town. The only opening was in the municipal garage, which serviced dump trucks and similar workhorse vehicles. But the engine repair section was fully staffed, so the shop foreman assigned me to the electrician's section, run by one Shalom Helfman. I came over, introduced myself, and told Shalom that I was here to assist him. Somehow this rubbed the fellow the wrong way. Perhaps he felt that I was sent to spy on him, or whatever, because he immediately set about making my life miserable.

I mentioned shortages, and this applied of course to all automotive replacement parts, in this case to batteries. When a car or truck battery no longer holds a charge, nowadays it is simply replaced. Not so in 1946, when batteries had to be *rebuilt*. Lead-acid batteries are made up of plates of lead and lead dioxide, with insulators in between. These are submerged in a solution of sulfuric acid and water, and sealed with tar, then slowly charged. To rebuild a battery, it had to be taken apart, drained, and the plates washed under running water. The process is then reversed, acid added, the whole resealed and the rebuilt battery trickle-charged. What this work - day in and day out - did to my hands I leave to the readers' imagination. And Helfman saw to it that I had a constant backlog, and I could not afford to tell him where to shove his bloody batteries.

Eventually I found work in a proper auto and truck repair shop. The British were leaving, war was on the horizon, and I was lucky enough to meet Felix, who had a little shop of his own across the street from where I worked. He took me in as a partner, and soon (November 1947) the Arabs attacked. As members of the Hagana, we were both called up, and had to close the shop. Felix specialized in diesel pumps that powered the IDF's tanks and armoured cars, and I was busy setting up mobile repair shops in IAF bases all over the country.

During one of the cease-fires, I was walking along Allenby Street in Tel-Aviv when who came walking towards me if not *Corporal* Shalom Helfman. His eyes bulged when he saw the sergeant's chevron on my sleeve.

Not a word passed between us. And I walked home on air!

8. BENNO

The war was over, but my parents waited in vain for any news of their families. By that time we knew what had happened to the Jews of Europe. The tension grew as lists of survivors became available through the International Red Cross. Alas, there were no familiar names. Then one summer day in 1945, a letter arrived out of the blue, from France: It was from my cousin Benno, who had survived long years in a German concentration camp. He had been liberated several weeks earlier, but was in such poor physical condition that he had to be transported to a convalescent center in France for rehabilitation. He was twenty-four years old. He remembered our address through all the eight long years of incarceration, and wanted to join us in Palestine as soon as possible. He arrived a while later, for a tearful reunion with my parents. He was a sorry sight to behold: still emaciated and stooped, a blue number tattooed on his forearm. One of his eyes bulged and was bloodshot from a recent blow from a rifle butt, and the shin of one leg was festering from an infected scar that ran from his knee to the ankle. It was all highly emotional, for as far as we knew, he was the only survivor. Our tiny apartment was stretched - we put up a cot in the kitchen for Benno - and he became part of the family.

Benno was not the quiet type. From the day he arrived, we spent our evenings gathered around the table or sitting on the balcony when it was too hot inside - and Benno talked...and talked. We listened in hushed silence. What we heard was beyond all belief, as he recounted the horrors of the Holocaust, before all the gory details became common knowledge. He had a strong need to share those horrors with people who cared, and we were a willingly captive audience. I will not go into too many details of what he related, just a few that are of particular importance. He had almost succumbed to dysentery and other infectious diseases. His leg wound was a result of frostbite. He was made to stand in the snow in sub-zero weather for many hours after the usual morning roll-call. He had no shoes, and his feet froze, one leg becoming permanently affected. By virtue of his exceptionally beautiful handwriting, he managed to survive his long ordeal. He was transferred to the camp office, where he was instructed, in true German fashion, to keep meticulously written records of all the deaths of inmates in the camp of Buchenwald. The causes were of course fabricated, but the names of the victims were correct. He brought this important document - a large volume - with him to Palestine. Today it resides in *Yad*

VaShem, the Holocaust memorial in Jerusalem. In time, he rented a typewriter and spent endless hours - for weeks on end - committing his gruesome memories to paper. (To this day these papers had not been edited or even looked at, although we offered to help. It might have been too painful for him to do so). He found work restoring old pianos and started to create a new life for himself.

We all kept checking the Red Cross lists of survivors, as well as those issued by the Jewish Agency. Then one day, Benno found a notice that his mother Anna was alive and still residing in Berlin. He immediately packed his meager belongings and returned to Berlin to reunite with her. By the time he got there, his brother Markus had resurfaced, and had also found Anna. Markus had managed to escape to Argentina. Their two sisters, Edith and Ruth, had disappeared. They were trying to escape with their husbands, but were caught at the border, never to be heard from again. Anna had remained in Berlin, hidden by a German lady friend, and survived all the heavy bombardments of the city in an underground shelter. My uncle Max had escaped with his wife to Antwerp, where they were caught and deported with the rest of the Jewish population. Bernard, the black sheep of the family, had escaped to Russia. On the way, he met another Jewish refugee, Raya. He was fifty years old when he married, and eked out a meager existence in Russia.

On my father's side, there was nobody left: as far as I would later find out, most Jews from Czestochowa in Poland were deported by train to Treblinka, to go up in smoke. According to my father's count, there were over one hundred members of his extended family unaccounted for, among them his mother, two brothers, two sisters, their spouses and children; his aunts, uncles and cousins and their offspring, who were numerous. My father walked around in a daze, but hardly talked about it. At the time I did not recognize the symptoms, but most likely they were another bout of the depression that haunted him throughout his life.

Benno, Anna and Markus returned to (pre-state) Israel as soon as they could, and tried to build a new life. They struggled desperately for quite a while, but could not make a go of it. Meanwhile, the German Government had begun a reparations program for the Jewish victims of the Nazi regime, which in their case was substantial. They returned to Berlin and started a new very successful venture in the piano business. ..

9. Ellie

We were hoping our second child would be a girl; our son Eitan often said he'd love to have a sister, and we were all delighted when Eleanor (soon to become Ellie) arrived early on a Sunday morning in Montreal. I hastened to wake Eitan, and we rushed to the hospital to meet the new arrival. Fast forward past the Oohs and Aahs to grade school, where shy little Ellie sat at the back of the room, trying not to be noticed. Before long, Marion became aware that something was wrong, and had a talk with her teacher. Ellie was then moved to the front row, and an amazing transformation took place: she soared right to the top of the class, and for several years was earning straight A's. The painfully shy blue-eyed little girl was now not afraid to perform in the Chinese dance from the "Nutcracker" (we filmed it), and was soon ready for music lessons. Her Saba (grandfather) gave her a white baby-grand piano, and she was anxious to learn to play and accompany her 'cellist brother, with Saba on violin and us on recorders.   The ballet lessons continued, now downtown. One day after picking her up after practice, we nearly ran over none other than the visiting Rudolf Nureyev!

Ellie received Music instruction from nuns in a nearby convent. We love baroque music, and listen to a lot of it at home. When Ellie's passion for the piano began to wane, we decided to bribe her with a harpsichord. She really went for that! We were about to move to California, so we found an instrument builder and arranged to have it delivered after our arrival there. The great revival of early music was at its height at the time and keyboard players were highly sought after, which gave Ellie a full schedule of high school and extracurricular activities. Because her grades were so high, she was allowed ate age 16 to attend university classes in her senior year in addition to those at University High, and upon graduation, was offered a scholarship for any UofC campus she chose. Ever independent, she opted for Eugene, Oregon, where one of her mentors, Richard Trombley, recommended she should continue her studies at Stanford U. in California. There she earned a Master's degree in early music practice. Following graduation, Ellie moved to San Francisco and tried to make a living with her harpsichord, and to keep body and soul together, she 'waitressed' for a while, until quite by accident, she responded to a help wanted ad placed by a property finance firm - and found her niche! She excelled at this work, and was soon being courted by other firms. Her job performance and reputation soared, she was news, and when starting work at a larger firm, word went around the finance community that 'Ellie was hiring.' How she managed to bring up five(!) children and manage two trans-continental moves is nothing short of a miracle.

Ellie at the keyboard

Ellie and family

Ellie foresaw the Wall Street crash and quit in disgust ahead of the storm. Next she went back to school, earning another Master's degree, this time as a nurse practitioner! Her older son Eugene had graduated from medical school with distinction, so she was keeping medicine in the family!

Drawing of Marion by Ellie's son Joel, a successful commercial artist

On a recent visit to Hawaii, Ellie contacted Richard Trombley, Ellie's music mentor from the University of Oregon, who was now living in Honolulu. It was a pleasure meeting him, and we subsequently published on Orion a recording of a recital he had played in Oregon. Ellie lives with husband Bill - an expert shiatsu therapist - and their cat and two dogs in Philadelphia.

10. Malibu Upstairs / Downstairs

In 1967 we moved from Montreal to Los Angeles, and settled in Westwood. I worked for a record company in Westwood Village, close enough to walk to (though I seldom did - California cities are not planned with pedestrians in mind). Our daughter was twelve at the time. The proximity of University High School and of UCLA influenced our decision to buy a little house on Ashton Avenue. The UCLA campus, an easy ten-minute walk up Westholme Avenue, provided a wealth of activities and entertainment.

As we got to know the Los Angeles area better, we were attracted to Malibu. As avid beach-goers since early childhood, we missed the ocean terribly during our long years in Montreal, with its interminable winters. Summer camping trips to Cape Cod were fun, but hardly filled our need for a life by the sea. The Santa Monica and Venice beaches were broad and surprisingly not crowded, yet not very interesting. Malibu, up the coast some twenty miles distance from Westwood, had far more varied beaches, which were virtually deserted most of the time.

We set our sights on Malibu Park, the area just past Point Dume. Only a few houses were scattered among the hills; it was wide-open country, and land was still relatively cheap. Yet it took us nearly ten years before were able to move there.

Marion had lined up a few realtors, and had done preliminary research for a few weeks. After the field was narrowed down to a few likely prospects, I joined in the house hunting on weekends. We looked at several homes on Point Dume and Malibu Park. Real estate agents called the area Pacific Riviera. I'm glad this pretentious name did not stick. Then we bought a big house on Busch Drive. It was barely a year old, on a half-acre of land. The young couple who had built it, we were told, could not afford the payments for the mortgage and building expenses. For us, this was not the first time as pioneers in a new area, far from town. Cities had spread out to envelop several of our former homes. This new house could not be seen from the street. It was on a hillside, and sat at the bottom of a very long driveway that ran between the two adjacent properties. On paper, the layout resembled a lopsided skillet.

The house was built over a three-car garage. Sliding glass doors fronted the length of the veranda, which faced the Pacific Ocean. The view from the balcony--as long as a bowling alley--was breathtaking. Inside, the layout resembled a railroad-car, with rooms opening off either side of the long hallway. It suited us perfectly, and had great potential. What I mean by this is that there was not a blade of grass growing on the place. We immediately made elaborate landscaping plans, including a swimming pool. This was the first house we owned that had enough land for fruit trees, in addition to ornamentals, lawn and a desert garden. We have a weakness for cacti and succulents of all kinds.

By the end of our second year in Malibu Park, most of our projects were completed. The trees we planted--about thirty different fruit trees--were still young enough to require constant attention. In spite of the poor soil quality, the only casualties were those whose roots were chewed by gophers. I soon came to view those critters as Enemy Number One. My next-door neighbor showed me how to set traps, and in time I acquired such skill that virtually none of them escaped.

Malibu soil is a mixture of decayed granite and adobe, a clay-like substance, impenetrable when wet, and hard as rock when dry. Its depth was only two or three feet over bedrock. Not much rain falls in Southern California, but when enough of it does, the earth can slip. Local building codes require houses to be solidly anchored into the rock. Roads and anything else--trees excepted--are another matter, as they can slide downhill. Our driveway was constantly developing new cracks.

Our great consolation was the swimming pool. By keeping it heated and covered when not in use, we were able to enjoy it all year long. Strong desert winds, called Santa Anas, blow regularly in the Los Angeles area. They are not so noticeable in the city, but in open country, they can be devastating. Winds pick up speed as they funnel down mountain passes and blow out to sea. Whenever a Santa Ana paid us a visit, the horizon over the ocean would turn yellow-brown. Gusts have been clocked at near one hundred miles an hour out our way. The damage can be easily imagined. Trees have been split in half, heavy roof tiles torn off and tossed into the air, and power lines knocked down. The smallest brushfire, unless put out immediately, can turn into a conflagration.

Sadly, there were disturbed individuals who waited for the right conditions, then set fires deliberately. A man who lived up in the hills was trapped by such a fire and died. The boy who set the fire was caught. Although technically guilty of manslaughter, he got off with a slap on the wrist.

Mother Nature in Malibu had a violent temper indeed. Stripped bare by the wind, leaves from our trees and neighboring ones, too--tons of them--ended up in the swimming pool. But I thought you said it was covered, people would say. Ha! The cover lifted off like a sail, and had to be retrieved from among the bushes. Even heavy lawn chairs took to the air during windstorms. The San Andreas fault runs the length of central California, and earthquakes are a regular, if infrequent occurrence. Mudslides after heavy rains blocked roads, and Pacific Coast Highway, the only link between Malibu and Los Angeles, was frequently closed. After one very bad slide, one had to make a forty-mile detour, through Malibu Canyon and the San Fernando Valley. Eventually, the roads department rerouted the highway around smaller slides, and erected 'The Great Wall of Malibu' at the site of the worst one.

We kept a running photographic record of these events. We call the magazines holding these slides the Disaster Files. A few years later, we can view them dispassionately, and even enjoy the survivor's experience.

Our verandah, as I mentioned, was as long as a bowling- alley. A good part of it was under the roof overhang. We didn't really need all that space out there. Marion had a brilliant idea: Why not enclose an area, to give us a solarium? And so we had a local contractor close off a space, the length of two rooms, with large windows and matching sliding glass doors. Jack, our contractor, was an easygoing fellow, a southerner who had settled in Malibu many years ago. When the work on the porch was finished, he had a suggestion:

'Do you folks need any more room?'

'Why, sure,' I replied. 'Never have enough space for all my junk.'

'Well, there's room enough for a small apartment down there, right under us.'

'You mean under the house?'

'Unh, hunh. I can build you a living bedroom and kitchenette, sort of a studio apartment. I can put in a bathroom, and you can put your mother in law in there. Or rent it out--pay for itself in no time.'

'Sure, if we charge a thousand dollars a month.'

'Nah, won't cost that much. Let me take some measurements and I'll give you a figure.'

The idea appealed to us. The new Pepperdine University campus was only a few miles down the road, and students were always hunting for off-campus lodging. A student could live downstairs rent-free, we reasoned, in exchange for services. He could do the heavy gardening, clean the pool, and bring in the mail and feed the dogs while we were away. It also meant we'd have someone on the premises at all times, a good idea in our dangerous neck of the woods.

Jack's estimate was reasonable enough. He agreed to let me help him, thus keeping costs down. It took only a few weeks, and the apartment was built. All that remained to be done was to paint the place and put in the carpet. There were two picture windows overlooking the garden. We had put in a small refrigerator and a two-burner stove. It gave Marion an excuse for replacing some dishes, pots and pans and cutlery, all of which went into the apartment. It was cozy. In size, it reminded us of the tiny apartment we rented when we were first married, and struggling to make ends meet. But what a difference in the setting!

GARDEN APARTMENT IN MALIBU PARK, IN EXCHANGE FOR YARD WORK. SINGLES ONLY, NON-SMOKER. CALL 457-3370. On my way into town, I placed this ad on the bulletin board at Pepperdine. By the time I got home a couple of hours later, there were five messages on the answering machine. It never occurred to me there would also be female candidates. The yard work, especially, was physically very demanding, so a girl would not be a good idea. Marion returned from her weekly shopping, and we were discussing the various messages while putting away the groceries. The telephone rang again.

'This is Bill March at Pepperdine. I called earlier and left a message. I'm a Law student...'

'Yes, I have your message,' I interrupted. 'I was going to call you.'

'I'll take it, if you'll have me,' Bill said.

'Well, not so fast. Let me catch my breath here.' I smiled at Marion; I like decisive people. 'Tell me something about yourself.'

'Well, like I said, I'm a Law freshman at Pepperdine. I've taught high school back in Indiana, and also coached the football team, before deciding to go back to school.'

'Football team?' I echoed. 'The ceiling in this apartment is pretty low. How tall are you?'

'Just under six feet,' Bill said. 'I coached a team of midgets.'

We had a good laugh over that, and Bill said he'd be over 'in a jiffy'. There were a few more calls before Bill arrived. I made careful notes of all the names, and promised to get back to everyone.

Bill drove up in an old Dodge van. A well-built, good-looking fellow of about thirty, he had a firm handshake and an engaging manner, if a bit on the loud side. Our dogs liked him, and it was mutual, a good sign. Can't fool dogs. I took him to see the apartment, and he was full of praise, even though it was still bare. Then we made a round of the grounds, and I told him what was expected in return for free lodging.

'No problem, this will be fun,' Bill said. 'You won't mind if I use the pool?'

'Of course not,' I hastened to assure him. We like to swim in our birthday suits. Anticipating such a situation, I had installed a little gate between the fruit orchard and the path to the pool. 'If this gate is closed, it means there's someone naked in the water.'

'I promise not to peek. When can I move in?'

'I still have to paint the place and put in the carpet.'

'That's alright--I'll do it!' Bill said.

'Okay, if you really want to. I've got the paint, also the carpet. I didn't want to put it in before painting.'

Bill left, returning a short while later with his belongings, which we put in the garage. Apologizing profusely, he then asked if I had the time to come with him in his van to Pepperdine. He wanted to pick up his motorcycle; would I mind driving the van back?

A motorcycle! Oh, boy. Bill didn't look the type. But I could say nothing; we were committed now. We took my car and I left him off at the university. When I heard the sound of the bike, I went downstairs. It was a huge, shiny Kawasaki, and looked brand-new. He obviously loved the machine. These toys are not cheap, so I made room for him in te garage, and told him he could park it inside at night. He said he was hoping I'd offer to do that, but dared not ask.

He did a good job of painting, and together, we laid down the carpet. Jack had built in a bed platform, for which we purchased a mattress. With shades on the windows and Bill's things in place, the room looked warm and lived-in.

We settled into an easy routine with Bill, who seldom had to be told anything. He was bright, energetic, and did his work cheerfully. He was also lively company, and we began to include him in dinner parties. Bill dressed casually, as is the custom in Malibu, but always managed to look sharp. I did not envy his laundry bills.

There was an abundance of cheap Mexican labor in Malibu, like the rest of southern California. Certain areas were 'slave markets' of sorts: every morning, men would be waiting, to be picked up by whoever needed a laborer or two for some menial job. They were desperate for work, and the competition for jobs was fierce. They would try to catch one's eye as you drove past them. If you slowed down, even for a stop sign, they'd be all over you, jabbering away. The lucky ones would pile into the employer's vehicle, which would turn around and head back home with *'Los escalvos felices.'*

Pick-up spots where Mexicans congregated were near the 'jungle', a eucalyptus grove off Pacific Coast Highway, where they slept. They were 'illegals,' with no papers or money. They slept in the 'jungle', under overpasses, even in restrooms on the beach. The Immigration people conducted periodical raids, carting off a busload of unfortunates to be sent south across the border. It made little or no difference. The following morning, there would be just as many of them in the same places. A week later, those who were deported would also be back.

The women fared a little better. There were many older homes in Malibu, whose garages were converted into mini-dormitories. As many as six or eight women would sleep there. In the morning, they fanned out all over Malibu, to work as domestics. They earned better wages than the men, who got minimal pay. These women had a 'union' of sort - a one-person institution, by the name of Manuela Siementhal. Manuela was about seventy years old. Somewhere in her genealogy there was German blood, obviously. No woman got a job without Manuela's intervention. She acted, in effect, as a madame, for maids.

Our neighbor Paul's help was called Socorro Delgado. One day we asked Socorro if she had a day a week to spare for us. Well, she'd have to think about it (i.e., ask Manuela). And so it came to pass that Thursday mornings, I'd drive over and pick up Socorro from the garage/room she shared with some other girls.

Socorro was a plump, pleasant-looking woman of about thirty. She told us she was married and had several children--the number varied whenever the subject came up. The children were back home in Sonora, Mexico, with her husband. When he was not in jail, that is. In his absence, they were cared for by her extended family. Her husband, she told us, had only one arm. That did not hinder him from fathering another child almost every time Socorro went home during the holidays. Children born in the U.S. were of course one hundred percent legal American citizens.

When she arrived, Marion offered Socorro a cup of coffee. As soon as I'd be out of the kitchen, she'd begin wailing: '*Ay, senora, yo tengo muchas problemas!*' Her husband, the one-armed wonder, had apparently shot someone and was behind bars. The children were sick. She gave a relative all her money to take home for her, but it was stolen by the *bandidos*. Or taken at the border. The stories followed a familiar pattern, and after a while all began to sound the same. But after unburdening herself, Socorro suddenly turned cheerful, and would start whistling and singing at the top of her powerful voice as she went about her chores.

We shared her services with a number of neighbors and friends, and Socorro stories made the rounds of barbecues and dinner parties. One of my favorites came from Paul, who was recently divorced. One morning Socorro, who had a key, let herself in. Paul was awake, but still in bed. Beside him was his girlfriend of the moment. Socorro innocently walked into the bedroom. When she saw the situation, she was terribly embarrassed. She quickly pulled her T-shirt up over her face and backed out of the room, bare-bosomed.

Dear old friends of ours, Janet and Jack, lived in the San Francisco bay area. We decided to rendezvous midway, and spend a weekend together in Morro Bay. We arrived late on a Saturday morning, and spent a relaxed afternoon together. In the evening, we all went out to dinner, and more good conversation. It had been a perfect day, and we looked forward to another. We parted at about ten, and went to our room in the motel. Marion turned on the news, and we were aghast: Malibu was on fire!

Without a moment's hesitation, we packed our few things, and bade our friends a hasty farewell. I kept the radio on during the two hundred or so miles to Malibu. This fire was a bad one, and still out of control. The updrafts from the fires generate their own windstorms, and dry brush and anything else combustible in its path simply had to burn out. Malibu residents are issued special identification passes; these got us past several roadblocks as we neared home. The smoke was thick, that unique smell of a brush-fire was everywhere. At the last roadblock we had to pass, the police advised we were proceeding at our own risk.

But we had not come this far just for the fun of it. I drove on, the orange glow of fires all about us. Fortunately, not from the direction of our house. The dogs were at the top of the driveway, and looked subdued and frightened. And there was Bill, standing on the roof with a garden hose! It was three A.M., and he had been there since early evening.

The fire was eventually brought under control. That Sunday, and for the better part of the following week, we were kept busy cleaning up after this near-disaster. Bill's well-intentioned rooftop vigil during the fire was of little practical use, since our water pressure was ridiculously low. Nevertheless, Malibu water rates were the highest in the County. We received Colorado River water, with assorted pollutants added along the way, and that at such low pressure. The water was so hard, it was almost impossible to work up lather, and the dishwasher was near useless. A softener had to be installed for the house, with a bypass for the garden, as soft water was not good for growing things. Bill took very long showers; it was a lifelong habit he was unable or unwilling to change. (Our son is like that too). So prospective tenants were now required to pay a small monthly fee for utilities.

It was still a bargain, so it came as no surprise that about a dozen people called after Bill graduated and left. Not all were students, and again, a few young ladies applied. We interviewed five or six, and accepted Tom, an Oregonian. He told us his father was a district judge. That sounded good. Soon after Tom moved into the freshly painted apartment, we took off for Hawaii. Honolulu had become our destination of choice. We even bought a little apartment on Ala Wai Boulevard in Waikiki. It was on the twenty-fifth floor, and had a spectacular view. At first, we used to visit Hawaii two or three times during the year. But that island is like a drug: The more you have of it, the more you want. We started coming oftener, and staying longer.

Our caretaker/tenants knew where a set of upstairs keys was kept in the garage. This was *for emergencies only;* otherwise they were not supposed to enter. When we returned from that trip, we found the back door unlocked, and the pool cover lay on the lawn, in full sun. The VCR was on, there ere rings where drinks had been placed, and the washer and dryer had been used. Tom 'thought it was okay' to use our house and have his friends over. We gave him two weeks' notice to clear out.

From there, it was all downhill, as far as student-tenants were concerned. During the few months that Tom lived downstairs, he managed to thoroughly trash the apartment. I suppose Bill, older and more responsible, had spoiled us. The succession of young men we had - we even tried a girl for a while - varied from slovenly to weird. None were even remotely satisfactory. Twice I had to unceremoniously throw tenants out. The situation was becoming critical. I was winding down my business activities, and we were often absent. We needed someone reliable downstairs.

LA FAMILIA SANCHEZ

Through our domestic Socorro, we got word to Manuela, Godmother to Malibu's Mexican community, that we were looking for a *couple.* We'd had our fill of flaky students and other 'weirdos.'

Jorge and Maria Sanchez had a kewpie-doll of a daughter, three-year-old Antonia. We thought long and hard about taking in a couple, finally concluding that the advantages outweighed the drawbacks. The little girl did not really make a difference. Although he had lived in Los Angeles for over ten years, Jorge's English was very poor, and Maria spoke not a word of it. We agreed she was to give us one day a week upstairs. Jorge's duties consisted of the routine maintenance jobs.

Had we finally found the solution?

They moved in on a rainy Friday. Soon we could smell beans cooking, even though the windows were closed. The odor of Mexican food (Jorge did the cooking) was to hang about for the next four years. I could smell it as soon as I entered the driveway.

Rain in Malibu is a curious thing. The forecaster could call for 'Showers, heavy at times, mainly along the coast.' Whenever that happened, it sounded wonderful, and like a farmer, I'd rub my hands in anticipation. It could indeed rain heavily in Santa Monica and all along 'The Malibu', but only a light sprinkle would be felt beyond Point Dume. That peninsula formed a barrier to precipitation coming from the south, however cloudy and threatening the skies might appear. Measurable rain came only from the northwest. Such was the storm we had the weekend the Sanchez family moved in. It began as a heavy downpour, and did not let up all night long. The following morning, it turned into a deluge. Nature is so wasteful: The shallow layer of soil could only absorb so much water. Rivers of mud ran into the ocean, which had turned brown halfway to the horizon.

I put on high boots and rain-gear, and went out to survey the (inevitable) damage. No major movement in nature could take place here without some damage. The garage was flooded -I expected that. Water had seeped in through the foundation, as usual. The dogs normally slept on the porch; on cold nights, they would opt for the warmer asphalt in front of the garage. When it rained, I'd leave a garage door partly open, and they slept inside.

After sweeping out the three bays with the large squeegee I kept for the purpose, I went into the garden. The dogs made a halfhearted attempt to follow, then went back inside. The little apartment windows were steamed over, the curtains drawn, and the lights were on. They're probably settling in, putting things away, I reasoned. I thought it strange that no sound came from inside. The rain did not let up all day, but had stopped sometime during the night.

We were concerned about the family downstairs. The day dawned glorious and cloudless. I would have expected them to show some sign of life by now. The shades were still drawn, lights still on. I knocked, but no one answered. Could they still be asleep? It was after eight. A little later, I knocked again, then tried the door. It was unlocked. The odor of sewage hit me as soon as I pushed it open. I was horrified at what I saw: The entire apartment was flooded! Sanchez and his family were nowhere in sight.

Getting a plumber on a Sunday in Malibu is never easy. While I waited for one to arrive, I looked around. The sewage had backed up through the drain in the shower stall. When I experimentally flushed the toilet, water rose again in the shower. So that was it: The toilet was blocked. When the plumber arrived, he confirmed my brilliant deduction. He pushed his long flexible cable down the toilet, and muttered it was not going through. Then one by one he began fishing out sanitary napkins and cornhusks, which had completely blocked the main drain. Maria must have been accustomed to using an outhouse in Mexico, and simply did not know any better. So whatever water they used, plus our showers and everything else upstairs, backed up into the apartment.

When he built the place, Jack wisely installed a sump-pump under the floor. This automatically drained any water that would collect inside the lower foundation wall during heavy rainfalls. After removing everything - carpet included -I washed out the apartment with a garden hose. I left all windows and the door open, with two fans running to speed up drying.

And where was Sanchez? They obviously panicked, and fled. Manuela did not know where they were, but was not upset in the least on hearing what happened. Nearly a week passed before they meekly showed up, bringing along a friend, to help explain. They began to apologize. That was not necessary, I told Jorge. As diplomatically as possible, I explained matters to Maria. I asked her to be very careful about throwing things into the toilet. She burst into tears, Marion consoled her, and we were back to where we started, before being so rudely interrupted.

Giv and Jorge

Jorge was a hard worker, never complained, and the 'folks upstairs and downstairs' got along harmoniously. Jorge usually finished his various chores by noon, and was then free for the rest of the day. One day, he came down the driveway behind the wheel of a huge, noisy '50s Buick rattletrap. We had never discussed such a possibility, since he told me that he did not have a California driver's license. We owned two cars, plus a camper and trailer, and space could be a problem, especially when we had company. I did not want to hurt Jorge's feelings, but had to take a firm stand, and told him he'd have to park the thing somewhere else, because, you know...Well, I need not have worried, because I never saw that Buick again, and forgot about it. Yet a few weeks later, he brought home another monster - this one an equally ancient *Lincoln!* He wanted to borrow tools to change the spark plugs and tune it up. Feeling sorry for him, I helped him out, but that was a mistake, and I had to remind him about parking elsewhere. Anywhere he liked, but not here...

I've no idea where Jorge went in his free time, but late one afternoon the 'phone rang. It was the Sheriff's office* calling, to ask if we knew Jorge Sanchez? Yes, of course - he lives here. Well, he's in trouble, I was told. What happened? He's in custody. He gave your name as a reference. To bail him out, you need to come to this office.

Oh, boy, I thought; that's all we need! I drove over, signed a warrant and wrote a check to guarantee that Jorge would abide by the laws of the land, including a driving instruction course and passing the test. "Our children are grown up and on their own," Marion commented ironically "and now we need *this!?*"

She need not have worried. We had sold the house and were moving to Hawaii in stages. Ellie had come down from San Francisco with a van and picked up a "bunch of stuff," as we referred to non-essential items - including some art and antiques. We had done the same earlier, loading up a Volvo station wagon that we drove to Toronto, leaving it with Eitan.

And the Sanchez's? True to form, one day they were simply gone. Vanished. And so ended a chapter, a unique way of life, rich in a variety of experiences. We gave our own farewell party, held a moving sale, and attended a round of dinners given by friends, ending with mutual promises of "keeping in touch"...

* Malibu is incorporated as a County, with its own sheriff's and other departments.

11. SHAGGY DOG

It was a fine spring Saturday morning in Malibu. The cool breeze blowing in from the Pacific was drying off the last traces of dew on the myoporum bushes that lined our driveway. I did not recognize the car that came down from the road. Two ladies were in it, and a large dog.

"We're looking for the owner of this dog. I think he's lost. And I think he's got a broken leg."

Now the lady was out of the car, and opened the back door. The dog limped out, dangling his right front paw just above the ground. He was huge, and was slowly wagging an enormously long and bushy tail. I had never seen and old English dog whose tail was not bobbed. This one certainly looked strange. I knelt down and scratched him behind the ears. One of his eyes was a warm canine brown, but the other eye was a very pale gray, and had a malevolent expression. He had no collar, and smelt awful.

"No idea," I said. "You might try a few houses up the road, on the left just past the corner. There's a family there that own a gray one just like this - same breed."

We hustled the fellow back into the car. He did not resist, but it was plain to see he was unhappy to leave. My eyes followed them as they left, and I felt a twinge of remorse. But we *had* a dog, and really didn't want or need another.

I had a letter I wanted to finish before the mailman passed by, so we went back into the house. A while later I went out to put the mail in the box. To my complete surprise, there was the dog, lying at our doorstep. I'll never know how he returned. He looked up at me with a pleading expression on his face: *Please* don't make me leave!

"Come quickly!" I called out to Marion. We knelt by him, and knew there and then that the fellow had found himself a home.

The commotion brought our pulik Giselle from the back of the house. She circled around, sniffing suspiciously. She was not happy with our guest.

The poor creature was clearly exhausted. I brought him some water, and he emptied the dish at once. I filled it again, and he just went on drinking. He was so parched that he drank a quart of water in one sitting. This was obviously a mature dog, but we had no idea what age. His teeth were yellowed, and a front one was chipped. On the back of his "knees" were large calluses. He had to be at least five years old. We discussed his age and how to go about adopting him. I put in a call to the friendly people at Animal Control. They told us the dog would be picked up, examined and given shots. He would be kept at the animal shelter for a week. If no one claimed him, he was ours. I assured the officer who came for him that we'd be happy to pay all fees, and please! make sure nothing happens to him. I knew that unclaimed animals were routinely destroyed.

During the following week, we took turns calling the animal shelter every day. They advertised lost and found animals in the pets column of the local paper, but no one claimed him. The vet told us the dog indeed had an old break in his leg which was never properly set and that had healed imperfectly. I could feel it when I touched the leg. But now that he was rested, he was back on all fours.

We were delighted! We decided to call him Effendi, which in Turkish is more than Mister, if less than a Pasha. Why the respectful title? Because this dog had Class! His manner was quietly dignified, and he bore himself elegantly in spite of his reduced circumstances. In appearance, that great shaggy maned head and huge paws were majestically leonine. Altogether, the vibrations between us were so positive as to be almost audible.

And so Effendi came home. We bathed and fed him, and then walked him around the grounds. Soon he was going about by himself, marking his new territory. He made a few friendly advances towards Giselle, whom we had spayed after she brought into the world a mammoth nine-puppy litter. But she turned away in a huff, indicating that she was going to have nothing to do with the newcomer.

Rusty, our neighbor Paul's Doberman, emerged from the bushes. "Here, Rusty!" I called out to him, "Come meet your new friend."

I should have known better. Before I knew it, they were at each other, snapping and snarling, the fur flying. By the time I managed to tear them apart, Effendi was badly mauled. Rusty had instinctively gone for his weak spot, and had savagely bitten his injured leg. We were terribly shaken, but Effendi quickly revved down. After cleaning and dressing his wounds - fortunately not bad enough to require surgery - he calmly lay down and took a nap. It was as though he was saying that such rude behavior is undignified and best ignored. But he did not forget Rusty's "welcome." Soon after the incident, Paul had a fence erected between our properties. The mere sight of each other would prompt bared fangs and raised hackles, and no day passed without the two enemies engaging in a snarling bark-fest on either side of the fence.

By the end of that first summer, it felt as though Effendi had always been with us, so comfortably did he fit in. He was an uncannily intelligent animal. One could sense he understood, and he soon acquired a wide range of commands. Giselle had grudgingly accepted his presence, and in return we lavished a lot of affection on her. Effendi showed no sign of envy or jealousy. When coyotes would yelp in the hills, all the dogs in the neighborhood would join in the chorus. With a regal toss of his great head, Effendi would pucker his mouth and send a long, ascending howl to the heavens. Giselle would respond with a soprano *obbilagto* to his baritone. We loved this singing and encouraged it - the sight and sound of them made us laugh to tears. Even a distant siren on the highway could trigger such a duet. If the sound was of a doubtful nature, Effendi would look at me questioningly. I could then get him going by howling myself, and we would then sing a trio when Giselle chimed in.

Most dogs in Malibu were on the loose, yet kept to their respective territories. But Giselle was an escape artist, and would vanish for days on end. She loved all people, especially children, but despised all dogs. To the end of her days, she remained a puppy at heart. She'd sit at the top of our driveway, waiting for the kids to pass by on their way to school, which was about a mile down the road. She'd cavort with them, and a good time was had by all. When she had had her fill of this fun, she'd come down the drive and resume her perch on the veranda. Occasionally, she'd follow the kids all the way to the school, and wander from one classroom to another, to the delight of everyone but the teachers! Her identification tag bore our telephone number, and we would get exasperated calls: "Your dog is here again. Please come and get it!" On one occasion, Giselle disappeared for almost a week. We searched frantically all over the neighborhood, but there was no trace of her. Nor did the animal shelter have anything to report. We had to assume the worst had happened: that she was run over, or had been killed by coyotes. We gave her up for lost, and were truly heartsick.

Then we received a call from a lady who introduced herself as Joan Morgan. She told Marion that Giselle had followed their son Murray home after school, and they simply adopted each other. She was allowed to sleep in his room, and they were inseparable. They expected the dog to leave, but Giselle, true to her gypsy ancestry, made no such move. We walked over to the Morgans and were happy to meet Joan and her doctor husband Richard. We became great friends with the Morgans, a thoroughly delightful couple with whom we had much in common.

Dogs were not allowed on the beach, but the injunction was largely ignored during the winter when it was virtually deserted. For the dogs this was pure delight. Here Giselle took the lead: Effendi had obviously never seen the ocean before and was at a loss, but she was a veteran. Since early puppyhood we'd been taking her for a romp, and it was enough to utter the magic word "Beach" to send her into a fit of excitement and expectation. One of her favorite sports was plunging into a flock of seagulls gathered on the sand, scattering the startled birds to the four winds.

When we'd go out to a restaurant or a dinner party, we invariably brought home a doggie-bag. Effendi, ever the gentle-dog, never poked his nose into Giselle's dish. She always gobbled up her food, while Effendi ate slowly, relishing each mouthful. I've concluded that the rumor about dogs choking on chicken bones is a myth, since they grind them down before swallowing. I remember a camping trip in Baja California: we were eating grilled fish by the campfire, dropping fins and bones to the ground. An emaciated dog appeared out of the darkness and hungrily feasted on the scraps.

I mentioned that Effendi never forgot nor forgave Rusty, the Doberman next door, for his vicious attack the day we brought him home. He bided his time until opportunity for revenge came, some five years later. Paul was out of town and our neighbor Betty was walking Rusty on a leash. Effendi pounced from behind, and literally tore the Doberman's back open. Poor Rusty took over one hundred stitches, and was subdued ever after. There were still stiff-legged, still-legged, bared-fang standoffs along the fence, to be sure, but these were silent encounters, and the fur no longer flew.

Malibu is horse country, where ticks, fleas and other vermin abound. It was quite a job keeping our dogs from being eaten alive, and we rarely allowed them indoors. They slept under the overhang, and when it rained, I'd let them into the garage.. Effendi was very clumsy, and when he scratched himself, he would go thump-thump-thump on the ground. Eventually we had to banish him from the veranda as the noise he made would not let us sleep. Once, when I had a bad cold, I went to sleep in the guest room at the other end of the house. The dogs always slept in front, but that night , I was awakened by the familiar sound of Effendi's thumping under my window. He knew I was in that room, and had posted himself under the window. Neighbors had suffered break-ins while their watchdogs slept, but we never had one in all the long years Effendi was with us. The mere sight of him kept mailmen and delivery people in their vehicles. I usually had to go down and "rescue" visitors from what they perceived as a threat to their safety.

It was inevitable that Effendi should have some romances. He had sired a litter of three by the lady sheepdog up the street. The pups were unmistakably his, black and white, while the mother was gray. One day when these pups were several months old, they came to visit Daddy. Giselle, true to form, was very inhospitable, but Effendi was plainly delighted. He lay down while his offspring swarmed all over him, pulling his ears and chewing his tail. Theirs had been bobbed, and they were adorably clumsy. We found ourselves looking at each other, the question unspoken...But there was no need for discussion: the answer was positively NO!

We never knew Effendi's real age. When he entered our lives, the vet told us he guessed he was somewhere between three and eight years old. Five seemed about right to us. I tried to lift him and get on a scale, subtracting my weight to find out how much he weighed. It was impossible; no lapdog, that!

All good things must sometime come to an end, however. We were vacationing in Hawaii when our housekeeper called with the shocking news that Giselle had drowned in the pool. Although she was trained to climb out, she was by this time sixteen years old. She was stone-deaf, nearly blind, and very feeble. We were devastated. So was Effendi. He refused all food for nearly two weeks, and we feared for his life. He only drank some water, and just lay around and moped. When food was put before him, he would sniff at it, then quietly get up and walk away. He slowly came around, but Giselle's death affected him profoundly. She was never nice to him, had constantly snubbed him when he tried to play, and even snapped at him. He could have easily squashed her, yet never so much as growled at her.

But Effendi was aging. He now sat down, or rather, collapsed with a grunt, and he had a hard time rising, pushing himself up painfully with his front legs. His hindquarters trembled when he stood, and he had to flop down in order to eat. Gone was the singing, for he could now hear nothing. Nor, I suspect, could he see very well. He was growing incontinent, and was tormented by incurable mange. The gentle giant who had enriched our lives for eleven long years was nearing his end. Our grandchildren had ridden him like a pony. If friendship had a flesh and blood embodiment, that was Effendi.

There are tears in my eyes as I write this. We kept putting it off, but the time came when it was no longer possible to wait...We firmly resolved to never own another dog. How could we? Dear Effendi, Dear Giselle - Thanks for the memories...

12. LUTHERSTADT WITTENBERG

The area south-east of Berlin, called the Altmark, is characterized by the extensive use of red brick in most buildings, including churches and some monumental cathedrals dating back to the early middle ages. The quaint medieval town of Wittenberg on the Elbe river is proudly called Lutherstadt Wittenberg because German Reformation leader Martin Luther (1483-1546) who settled here about 1521 taught, preached and is buried at the St. Marien Evangelical church. The church also boasts a splendid altar and numerous paintings by no less an artist than Lucas Cranach the Elder (1472-1533). Cranach was the court painter of Count Friedrich the Wise (1486-1525), and had served as the town's mayor. This church also perpetuates one of the vilest, most disgusting slanders ever committed in the long history of Jewish persecution in Germany.

At this point, I believe a word about what brought us here is in order. Sixty years ago - almost to the day - Marion and her family left her native Berlin, leaving everything behind in their flight to safety in Israel. They left, she remembers, the day after Rosh Hashana, 1935.

An invitation from the City of Berlin arrived earlier that year, a gesture of reconciliation to former Berliners to spend a week as guests - a spouse or other companion were included in the invitation - of the City. The date of the visit in late September overlapped Rosh Hashana.

That eventful week was typically well planned. However, since we were in Germany for the first time since reunification, we wanted to see the eastern part, which had been inaccessible before. We mapped out our own itinerary that included medieval towns and walled cities of historical interest that had not been reduced to rubble, as was for example Dresden. It was inevitable that our journey along those cobbled byways, in use since Roman times, would become a retrospective of antisemitism, that ages-old malady...

*****

In the early days of his religious activities, Martin Luther advocated universal tolerance and brotherhood, and condemned the long-standing practice of persecuting the Jews. He nevertheless nurtured the belief that after hearing his message, many Jews would convert to Christianity. Some Jewish theologians sympathized with Luther's reformist philosophy, even to the point of hoping that it could lead him to return to Judaism. With the passage of time, however, and to Luther's chagrin, the opposite occurred: The stiff-necked Jews (*"Am ksheh oref"* - Luther had an excellent command of Hebrew*)* refused to abandon their faith and accept his message. His kindly attitude towards them gave way to increasing impatience and irritation, and eventually to open hostility, culminating in vituperative attacks in sermons and pamphlets published in his later years. Never known for subtlety, Luther at this stage became a common rabble-rouser, resorting to medieval polemics altogether out of keeping with his previously attained stature as a respected theologian.

This is most painfully evident in the pamphlet entitled *On The Shem Hamphoras(h)* of 1543. A sandstone bas-relief had been placed in 1305 on the southeast corner of the St. Marien Evangelical church in Wittenberg. It depicts a Jew copulating with a sow suckling her young, the scene surmounted by the words "Shem Hamephoras", the name of God, which may not be uttered by pious Jews.

This ancient mockery of the Jews has a long and shameful history. Since the 12th century, the ugly sow theme had been widely used inside and on the exteriors of European churches. Not only was every tourist who passed through Wittenberg made aware of it; Martin Luther elaborated on it extensively in his 1543 polemic, using its very existence as precedent and justification for his vile outpourings.

Shortly before his death in 1546, Luther preached a sermon called *Admonition against the Jews,* recommending measures ranging from forced labor to confiscation of property and outright expulsion. Since Luther was an influential force in Protestant ruling circles, his advice was heeded and widely implemented. Through the ensuing centuries, his vicious denunciations have proved fuel for anti-Semitism, culminating in Nazi Germany's "Final Solution".*

In November of 1988, a memorial was unveiled on the south side the church, roughly at the foot of the "Jewish Sow". An explanatory pamphlet available in the church reads in part: ANIMOSITY TOWARDS THE JEWS HAS HAD A LONG TRADITION IN OUR CHURCH...HOW IS IT POSSIBLE THAT THIS (SHAMEFUL) BAS-RELIEF HAS REMAINED UNTOUCHED FOR SUCH A LONG TIME?"

A modernistic monument by Mecklenburg sculptor Wieland Schmiedel is a plaque placed on the ground, to signify that something shameful is buried underneath. Two intersecting lines form a cross, so devised that when it is stepped upon, something akin to molten lava appears to be oozing from the crevices of the cross. Psalm 130 (*Mima'amkim kra'aticha*) in Hebrew lettering runs the length of the two sides, and the entire is surrounded by the following text, the work of author Juergen Rennert of Berlin: THE TRUE NAME OF GOD, THE REVILED SHEM HAMPHORAS, HELD BY JEWS UNUTTERABLE FOR CHRISTIANS, DIED WITH SIX MILLION JEWS UNDER THE SIGN OF THE CROSS.

It is perhaps significant to note that both artist and author belong to another generation, having been born in 1942 and 1943, respectively. A mini-exhibit inside the church shows a close-up of the bas-relief and events surrounding it, sparing visitors the trouble of craning their necks to see it up on the wall outside. For there it remains. It is, after all, a tourist attraction.

* During out tour of Berlin, our guide, a very intelligent and sensitive young German lady who spoke fluent Hebrew - having studied at the University of Jerusalem - pointed out to us the Berlin Marienkirche. She told us the following: On a certain date during the 12th century, it was discovered that the Host had been stolen from the church. Perhaps the theft was merely a pretext, but a large number of the local Jews were rounded up and collectively accused of the crime. They were all condemned to be burned at the stake in front of the church. Two of the Jews who agreed to convert were granted the privilege of being beheaded as Christians.

13. A Tuna Auction In Hilo

Even by Hilo standards, the rain that fell during the night was especially heavy and sidewalks still glistened. The tuna catch was good, and the fishermen were bringing in their haul early. By 6:30 A.M., several dozen magnificent specimens of yellow-fins were unloaded off the boats or brought in by truck. The fish were hoisted by their tails and weighed; some tipped the scale at 150 lbs. Then they were hauled with gaffs, beginning with the largest ones, and laid out on rows of great white pallets. An inspector from the Fisheries Department examined the tuna and placed a label on each fish. The inspector was followed by a man who took core samples by plunging a thin metal tube under the fin, then carefully laying out the suctioned meat on a sheet of paper. Buyers were then able to determine flavor and quality by the color of the sample.

In addition to the tuna, there were also squid, weighed in lots of about 15 lbs. each, and put in boxes covered with ice. There were also a half-dozen 3 foot-long Mahimahi, and a quantity of smaller fish. Everyone was working furiously against the clock. The fish had to be sold, delivered, prepared or packaged for sale, all within a relatively short time to preserve freshness. The workers wore back-supporters over their aprons, and sloshed about in knee-high rubber boots. Everything was constantly being hosed down, and the auction area and its adjacent fish-market were remarkably odor-free.

The throng of onlookers - locals and tourists - crowded around the roped-off overhang, vying for good vantage-points. The auctioneer appeared - a big, burly fellow with a Fu-Man-Chu moustache and goatee - ringing a huge bell that was loud enough to waken the dead - and shouting HEY! HEY! HEY!

The buyers approached the first row of pallets, and the auction began:

"Who give me two dollah?", he shouted.

There was no answer.

"One seventy five?"

Silence.

"One fifty then!"

One of the bidders raised an eyebrow.

'HEY!" exploded the auctioneer, "I've got one fifty. Who give me one seventy five?"

Another buyer inclined his head, ever so slightly.

"HEY!" bellowed the auctioneer, "I've got one seventy five! Who give me two dollah?"

The action was heating up. Each time someone indicated assent, the auctioneer would shoot a forefinger and thumb at him and shout "HEY!"

As buyers started bidding against each other, the accusing forefinger and thumb waved quickly back and forth between them, and explosive "HEY!s" punctuated the narrative. When all the tuna were sold, there was some keen bidding on the squid. One man lifted some of the slimy creatures for a closer look, and ended up buying the lot of six boxes. There was hardly a fight over the smaller fish, but fierce bidding erupted over the Mahimahi, that fetched what I thought was a very low price for such a delicious fish. At the present rate of inflation, these prices seem like a faraway dream...

Then the buyers claimed their goods, and the tuna were hauled by gaffs in their gaping maws across the sidewalk to the waiting trucks. After all the deliveries were made, the whole area was hosed down once more. The entire spectacle lasted a little over an hour.

14. Da Regulahs

Just outside Waikiki, there is a peninsula called Magic Island. For us– Marion and I—the magic lies in the kilometer-long natural swimming pool enclosed by the reef west of Magic Island. MAGIC, it so happens, is an acronym of our names, and it was swimming that had brought us together fifty years ago. True, we might stray once in a while and visit another beach, or the presence of jelly-fish might occasionally force us to use (shudder!) a 'sweet-water' pool for our laps. But Ala Moana Beach is our regular year-'round haunt, rain or shine.

Most of the people we see at the beach are retired seniors like us . I'm sure they observe us with the same natural curiosity common to people at leisure. 'This couple,' I imagine Someone A telling Someone B, with a nod in our direction, 'Have been coming here for as long as I can remember. Their routine never changes. They arrive around nine, sit under that coconut tree there, and read for a while. Then they go jogging in the water, and after that they swim all the way to the wall - see that buoy over there, by the antenna? She walks back, he swims both ways. If it rains, they sit under umbrellas, but the routine is always the same.' (Aqua-jogging, I firmly believe, is one of the finest forms of exercise. Sure, it looks funny, and induces great fits of giggling by Japanese tourists, especially when I run backwards. But over time, we see more and more people doing it.)

Well, so much for us. In no particular order, here are thumbnail sketches of some other regulars we've been observing. We know only a few of them by name, and hope that those who might recognize themselves won't take offense at the names we've invented for them- bearing in mind it's all in the spirit of good fun.

Laughing Boy is a very tall, thin man in his eighties, whose skin hangs from his spare frame in folds. Phil the lifeguard told us the man had once weighed one hundred fifty *kilos*. When for some reason he lost a lot of weight, his skin, no longer elastic, could not return to its normal state. When we did not see him for a while, Phil (the lifeguard) told us he now came for his swim before sunrise, and is gone by the time we arrive.

Kamikaze must be the most doggedly determined jogger in Honolulu. We go to the beach on even days of the week, but sometimes are forced to change the schedule. Yet we never miss seeing **Kamikaze**, who runs in the deep sand every day of the week (I hope he rests on the weekend!). He runs all the way to the wall, back to the tip of Magic Island, and back again. Around and around, he keeps this up for hours: bathed in perspiration, his head hanging to one side, he grimly jogs on, oblivious to his surroundings. We regulars always exchange greetings, wave at each other and make the Shaka sign. Not so **Kamikaze**, who is too busy being what seems to me as distinctly unhappy.

For years, **Wolfgang** would walk the length of the beach, back and forth for hours on end. He was dressed for maximum protection from the sun: white slacks and long-sleeved shirt, and a large floppy hat that left most of his face in dark shade. We always exchange greetings; **Wolfgang** has a surprisingly deep voice for someone of just average size. Imagine our surprise when one day we saw him *jogging* - something we'd never seen him do before. And he was wearing shorts, too! Not long after that, he surprised us again by metamorphosing into - a lifeguard!

Sammy was dressed and looked like a tourist--which he could not be, since he obviously lived here. What distinguished this elderly, somewhat overweight fellow was the band-aid he always wore in the middle of his back. His shirt rolled up under his arm, he'd walk the length of the beach with a transistor radio held to his ear, and never failed to touch each and every coconut palm he passed. It's been a long time since we've seen him, but these old regulars have a way of disappearing for months on end - and then re-appearing just as suddenly.

Another man who is always dressed and wears shoes(!) to walk in the sand is **Tamevateh**, a middle-aged man we cannot figure out. He adheres to a very strict dress code: white long-sleeved shirt, and navy slacks rolled up to mid-calf. For years, we've never seen him wear anything else. He carries a cap that he seldom wears, and walks the length of the beach a couple of times, regardless of how hot the weather might be. Why, sir, don't you dress more comfortably? I wish you'd tell us!

Sam Seegar (Sam is his real name) is the oldest member of a group that meets at the lifeguard tower every morning. They don masks and fins, and swim slowly up-shore, where they are met by one of the ladies in the group. Then they all walk back, carrying on a lively conversation. I often pass them in the water, and we wave at each other. By the time I've swum to the end and back, Sam and his friends, dried in the sun by the lifeguard's tower, are ready to leave. Then he lights up a cigar (smoking on the beach is prohibited). We always have a little chat. 'Yo missus, she go slow but boy she swim fast!' Sam commented on Marion's long, easy strokes. For a few weeks a while back, Sam was absent. When I asked about him, a friend told me he underwent cataract surgery and had to stay out of the water for a few weeks. I was happy to welcome him back. Shortly after his return, he celebrated his ninetieth birthday. Then he went absent again. I found out that Sam, who lives in the Kaimuki area, was no longer comfortable driving to Ala Moana. When I suggested we could pick him up on our way in from Hawaii-Kai, the friend said others had made similar offers. Ever independent, Sam declined: if he couldn't make it on his own, he preferred to take a walk around the block at home instead.

What we call 'The Parliament' consists of a group of regulars, firmly anchored by two individuals, **Schleiger** and **Hippo**. Their spot is the bench on the sandy sidewalk, hard by the showers across the street from the park. **Schleiger,** who looks like a retired wrestler, is a well-spoken, articulate person. A while back, he grew a short beard that lent him a very distinguished appearance. He and **Hippo** undertook the Sisyphusian task of growing a lawn in their area, which they take turns watering. Perseverance paid off, though, and there is actually a grassy area now by the bench. They only wade in the water - I have never seen them swimming. **Hippo** and **Sam** often join them at the bench, and what sounds like lively debates go on for hours. **Schreier's** voice is high-pitched, and carries over a great distance. He exchanges lively comments with the park's maintenance men and other friends who pass by. At Christmastide, Hippo brings a ukulele and they have a little song-fest.

It's amusing to watch **DOM** (Dirty Old Man), who earned his moniker by ogling all female forms lying on the sand. Like **Sam Seegar** and his group, **DOM** swims a couple of beach lengths. On his slow, shuffling jog back, fins tucked under his arm, he weaves a zig-zag path along the beach from one sunbathing lady to another, craning a stiff arthritic neck in a comically obvious manner.

PENGUIN is the name we gave a middle-aged-to-elderly lady, who is so heavily swathed in clothing it's hard to guess her age. We usually see her slowly waddling (like a penguin) in the sand when we arrive at our usual spot, and almost always coming back – a little over an hour later, as we leave. We tried to greet and wave at her, but she never reacts.

There are of course many more fascinating denizens of this, and probably any other popular beach. It's a wonder we get any reading done!

Much of this belongs to the distant past. More recently, having attained "Regular" status, we've been included in the annual luau held under the trees at the southeast corner of the park. This is a typical Hawaiian "feast and fress" bash, to which all attendees contribute, be it food, music and/or dancing. After the last one, an enterprising member brought a movie camera and filmed a short movie entitled "The Morning Crew". We enjoyed watching it a while later on U-Tube. Try it!

***

The following *is an excerpt from a piece* by Chris Higgins that appeared in the Valentine's Day, 2000 issue of **EAST HONOLULU** newspaper.

15. "A Republic Of Two"

They met at the tender age of sixteen. World War II was raging. The world looked bleak. Countries were crumbling, and hatred was spreading violently out of control with each new conquest, a rapidly burning wildfire consuming everything in its path. And yet, amid such destruction, love blossomed, unencumbered by the oppressive surroundings - and a Valentine's love story began...

Asked for the secret of their success through thick and thin in the ensuing decades, The couple answered: "Not everyone is fortunate enough to meet when they are so young, and grow up together; it's a republic of two - there's no royalty and no aristocracy - it's 100 percent equality."...The couple concentrates on the good memories, and they don't look back a lot - they enjoy the present. They keep a positive outlook on life. " We survived it all, we're here and we're happy," Marion said. From that fateful Valentine's Day in 1942, to Valentine's Day, 2000, they have endured. The wars ended. Countries rebuilt. Life went on. And through it all, true love did not waver.

Printed in the United States
By Bookmasters